A STORY ABOUT KINDNESS + POSITIVITY

I choose yellow

WRITTEN BY

EMILY CASEY + ALYSSA KING

PICTURES BY

EVIE GERMAN

For Emily

You taught me that you do not need to use lots of words or big, fancy words to have a voice and share your message with the world. The wordless language that you created using kindness, positivity, and love will speak volumes for years to come. I love you more than words can describe.

A.K.

For Asher, Avery, Geoff, and Pam

E.G.

People say, "Don't judge a book by its cover."
So why do we do that to one another?

On the outside, I'm labeled by what others see;
But they don't realize that's only one part of me.

When I feel sad, and words leave a bruise,

I tell myself, "I have the power to choose."

Today I won't be anything I don't want to be.

I'll only be, totally, one hundred percent me.

Today I'll be YELLOW – so LOVELY and BRIGHT;
Happiness glows in my warmth and my light.

Today I'll be YELLOW – I'll be LOUD and BOLD;
I'll spread love like sunshine with my ♥ of gold.

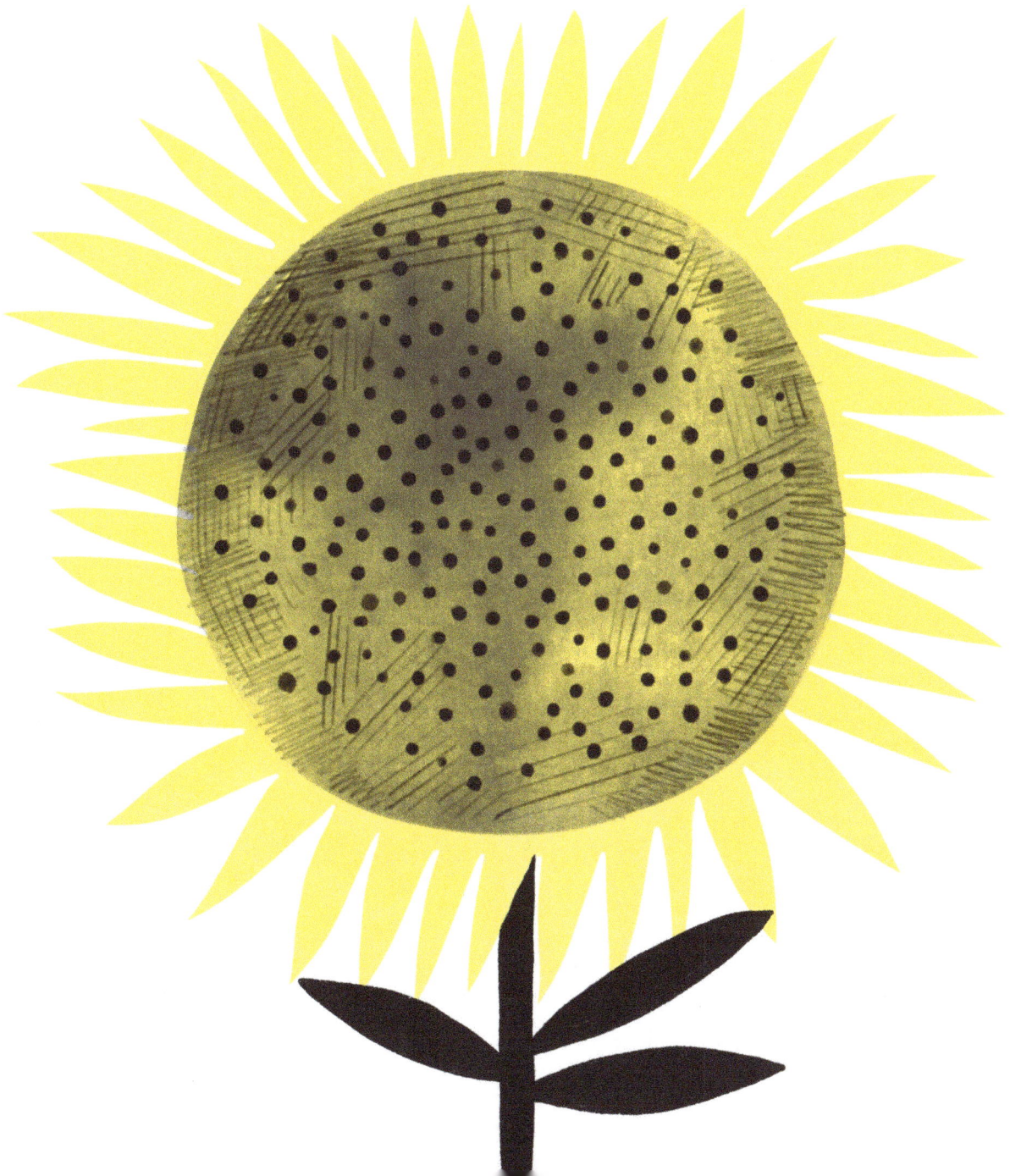

BOSSY

shy

When others use words that
bring me down, when they try to
hurt me or make me frown...

ROWDY

SPACEY

fidgety

I'll tell myself, "No, no! That cannot be! I can be anything – and I choose to be ME."

Today I'll be YELLOW - STRONG and COURAGEOUS.

I'll use my laughter; I know that's contagious!

YAY ha ha HA HA ha HA YAY YAY HA HA YAY HA Ha

Today I'll be YELLOW and CHEERFUL and SWEET...
I'll see only the best in all whom I meet.

YOU'RE AWESOME

I'll lead by example, be a friend to all;

I'll never say things that make others feel small.

BE KIND

I'll try to show people who don't understand,
It's better to be kind and lend a helping hand.

Kindness has the power to show love and make friends. It can help put negative labels to an end.

ATHLETIC

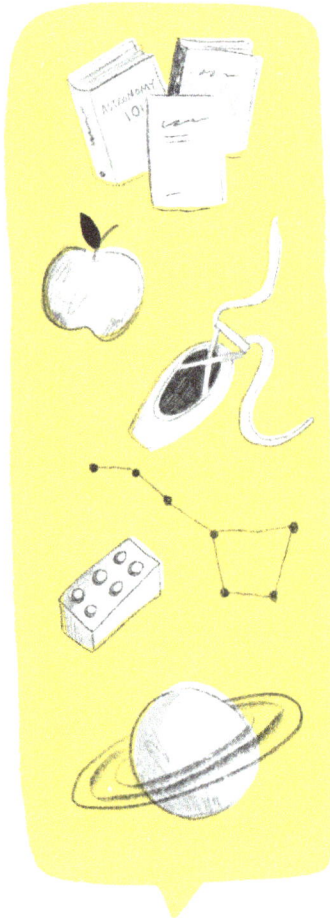

BRIGHT

PASSIONATE

CREATIVE

YAY

CONFIDENT

Next time I'm labeled by what's on the outside, I'll remind ME – I'M THE ONLY ONE TO DECIDE.

So, I choose to be YELLOW.

That's MY superpower, I think.

WHO KNOWS?

Maybe YOUR superpower is PINK!

I Choose Yellow is about a young girl, Emily Marie Casey, who tackled life's challenges with positivity.

Emily lived in Mason, Ohio. She lived a beautiful life of courage and love for 18 years. Emily and her companion Alyssa were best friends and a dynamic duo who enjoyed going on adventures. During their time together, Emily shared her love of dogs, friends, family, soccer, hot dogs, reading, and all things yellow. But the most important thing Emily shared with Alyssa was the message she wanted to share with the world.

This book was written to help advance Emily's lifelong mission of changing the world by CHOOSING to act with kindness and by encouraging small acts of kindness by others. Emily did not let her inability to speak silence the message she wanted to share with the world, so she made her own language—"Emily language." Yellow was her favorite color and Alyssa's favorite word in Emily's vocabulary. It had a special meaning: it stood for positivity, kindness, and courage. Emily and Alyssa wrote *I Choose Yellow* together; Emily was the author, and Alyssa was her scribe.

www.ingramcontent.com/pod-product-compliance
Lightning Source LLC
Chambersburg PA
CBHW040314100426
42811CB00012B/1442